TREBLE CLEF INSTRUMENTS

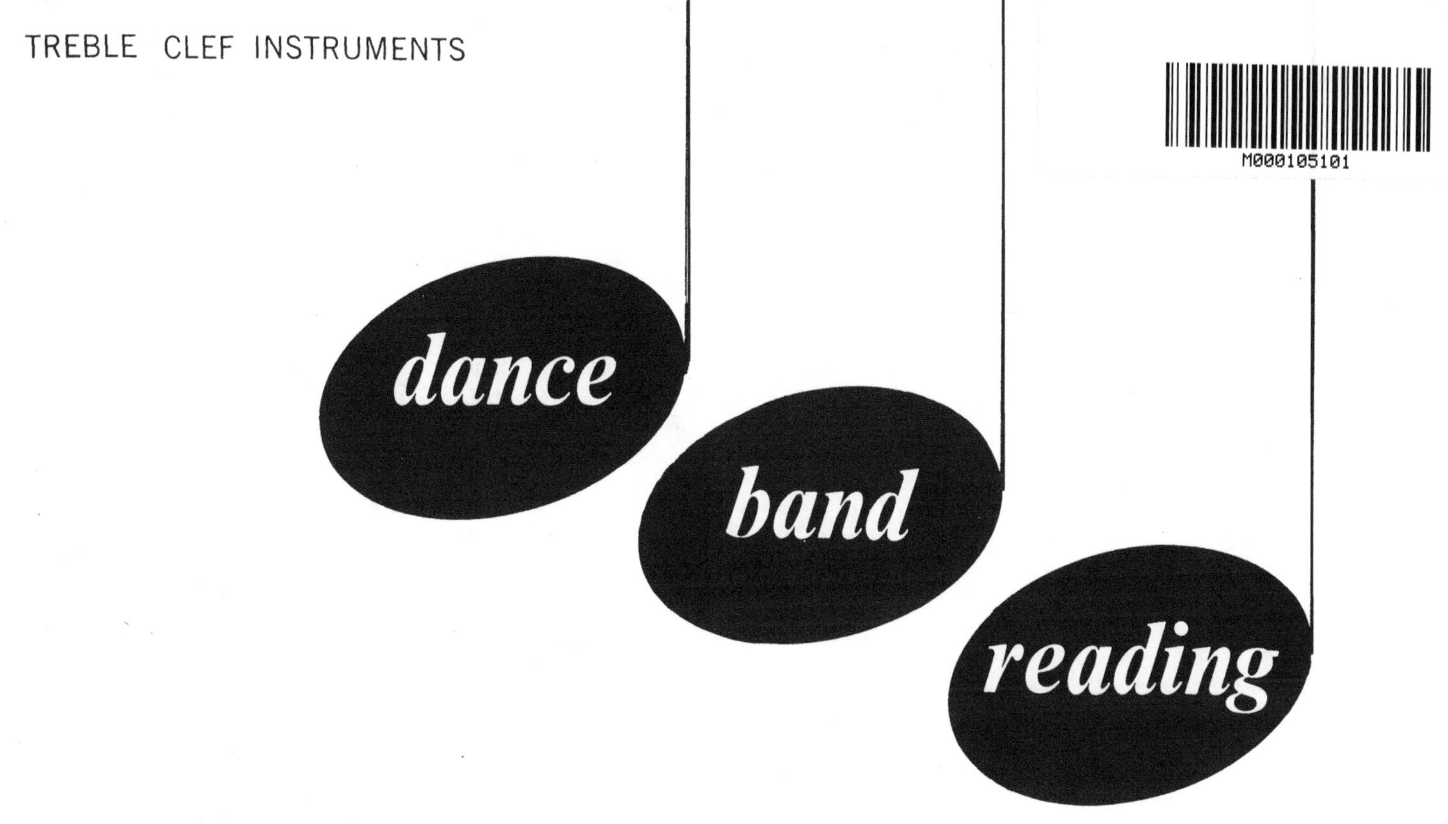

dance band reading and interpretation

The Basic Concepts Of Dance and Jazz rhythms.

ALAN RAPH

DANCE BAND READING AND INTERPRETATION

This book is for those instrumentalists who would like to familiarize themselves with, and become proficient in playing today's dance and jazz rhythms with a correct conception.

The book's basic principle combines a group of FIVE comprehensive rules (p. 3) to be learned and applied to dance and jazz parts. Many examples of the most commonly used rhythms are presented, explained, and used in context with figures and etudes typical of actual dance band music.

For additional reading skill the examples and etudes throughout the book are presented in a variety of keys. As in dance arrangements, this book utilizes the full range of most wind instruments.

CONTENTS

BASIC RULES

Here are FIVE basic rules to the understanding and interpretation of dance band music. They are to be studied and applied to the examples, figures, and etudes throughout this book. Special interpretation markings and exceptions to these rules, will be explained as they occur.

It will be of great help to use this page as an overall guide to the pages that follow. Check back frequently, and pay particular attention to rules 1, 4, and 5.

- EXAMPLES -

WRITTEN PLAYED

Rule 1. *Quarter-notes* are played *short.*

Rule 2. Any note *longer* than a quarter-note is given its *full* time value.

Rule 3. *Single eighth-notes* are played *short* (and often accented).

Rule 4. *Lines* of *eighth-notes* are played with a *"lift"* in a long-short manner, the same as eighth-note triplets.

Rule 5. *Two* or *more eighth-notes* are *slurred up to a quarter-note (or its equivalent). Whatever follows* is *started by tonguing* (T).*

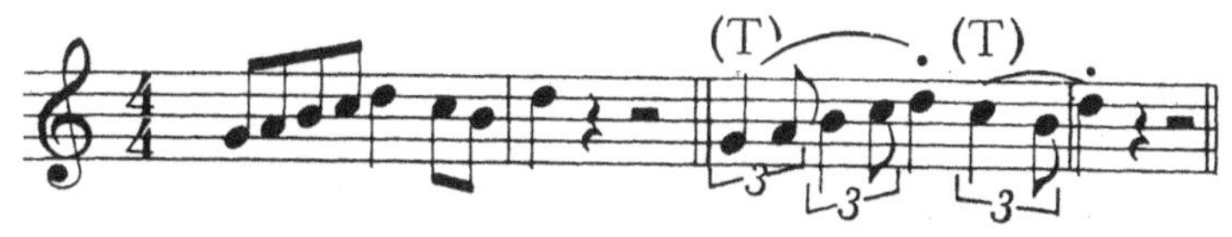

*On stringed instruments: (T) = new attack.

APPLY THESE RULES TO ALL OF THE FOLLOWING EXAMPLES, FIGURES, AND ETUDES.

Tempos in this book, when not specified, should be medium bright: (♩=126-144). Interpretations at other tempos will be presented and explained later.

SEE GLOSSARY (PAGE 43) FOR DEFINITIONS OF TERMS USED.

EXAMPLE

(Eight bar melody; Apply rules 1-5)

WRITTEN
PLAYED
Rule 1.
Rule 2.
Rule 3.
Rule 2.
Rules 4 & 5-

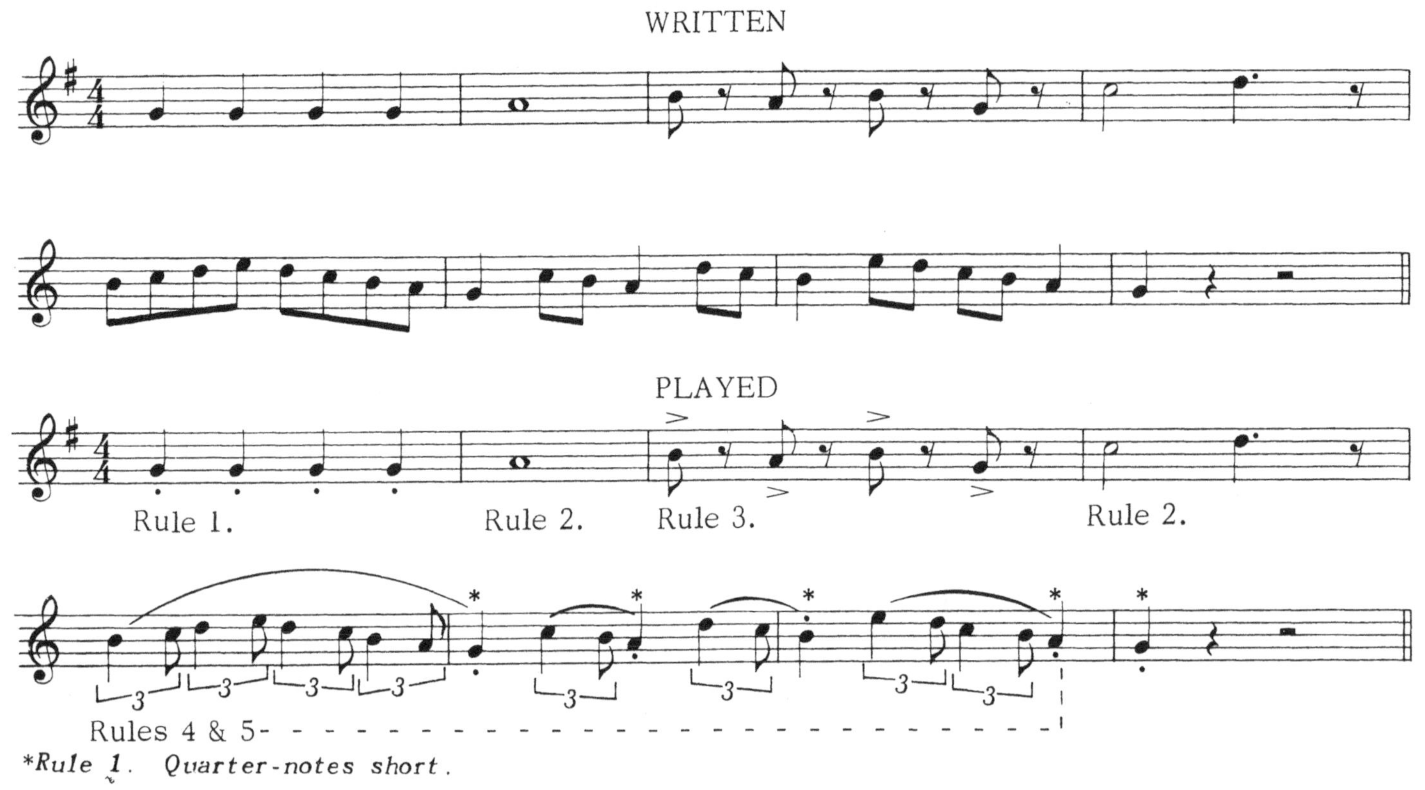

*Rule 1. Quarter-notes short.

PRIMER FOR ONE BAR FIGURES

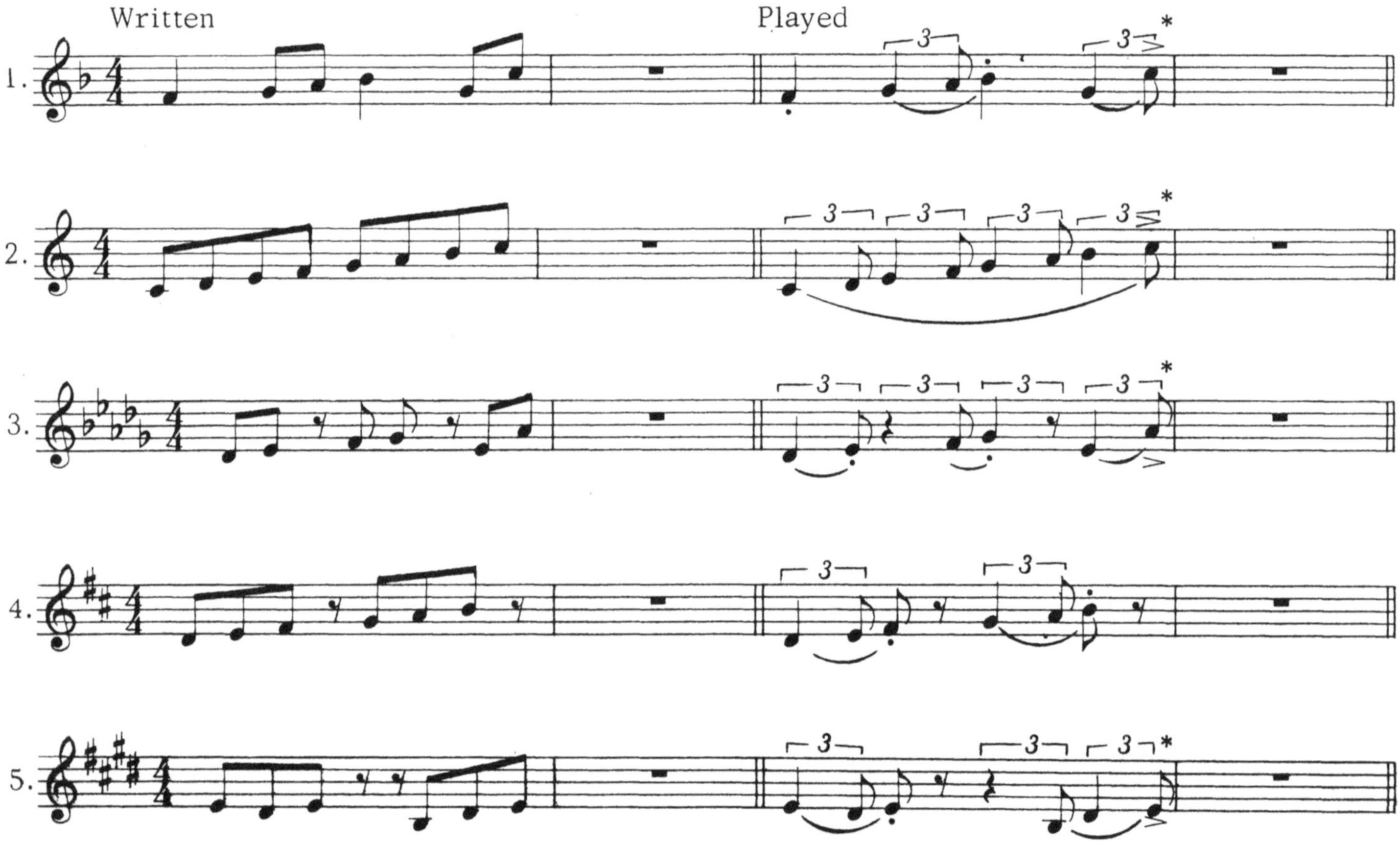
Written
Played
1.
2.
3.
4.
5.

*The last eighth-note (in numbers 1, 2, 3 & 5) anticipates, and should "feel like" the down-beat of the following bar. This is *why* it is accented.

ONE BAR FIGURES

Repeat each of the above figures several times.

Most dance band rhythms can be "broken-down" into basic eighth-note triplets. Use the KEY on page 44 for difficult figures.

FIVE ETUDES

(Mixing all of the one bar figures)

Notice that key signatures - typical of dance band parts - occur only once at the beginning. Key *changes* are marked as they take place.

See Glossary (page 43) for explanation of tempo markings (Medium bright, Medium slow, etc.).

The number above each measure indicates the one bar figure (page 5) being used.

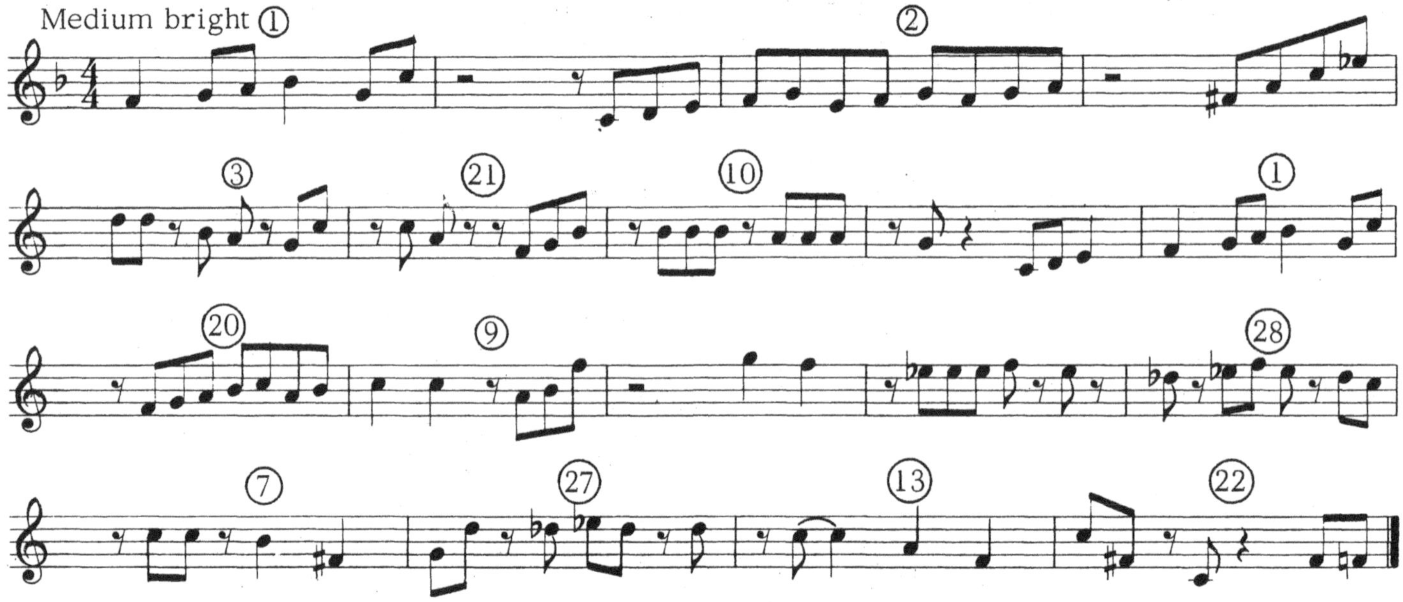
Medium bright
I
1
2
3
21
10
1
20
9
28
7
27
13
22

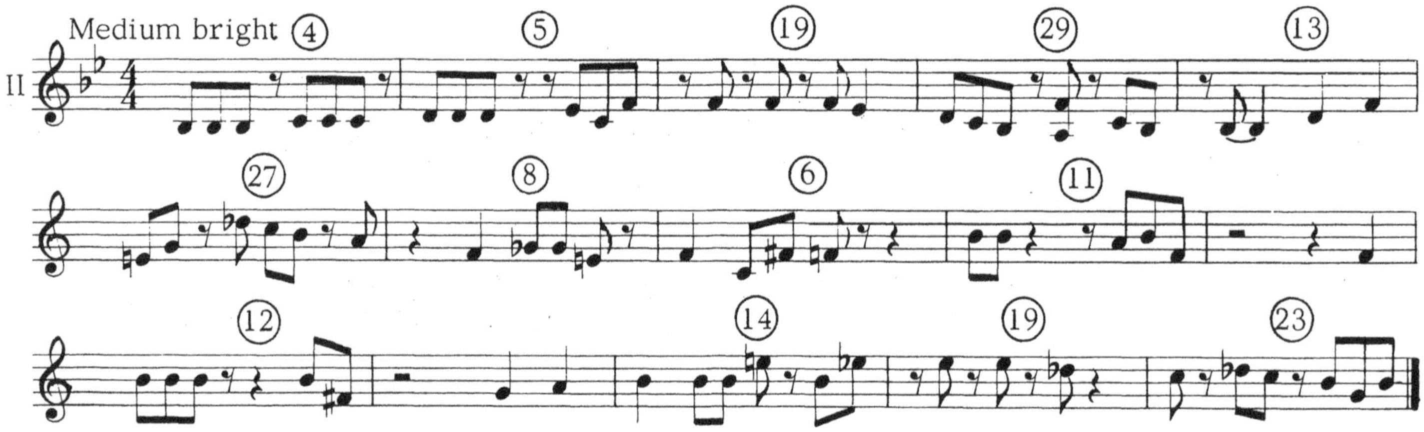
Medium bright
II
4
5
19
29
13
27
8
6
11
12
14
19
23

The following etude (III) is at a slower tempo. Make the note values slightly longer, and put more "weight" on isolated notes.

Medium slow
III
15
16
17
25
24
15
18

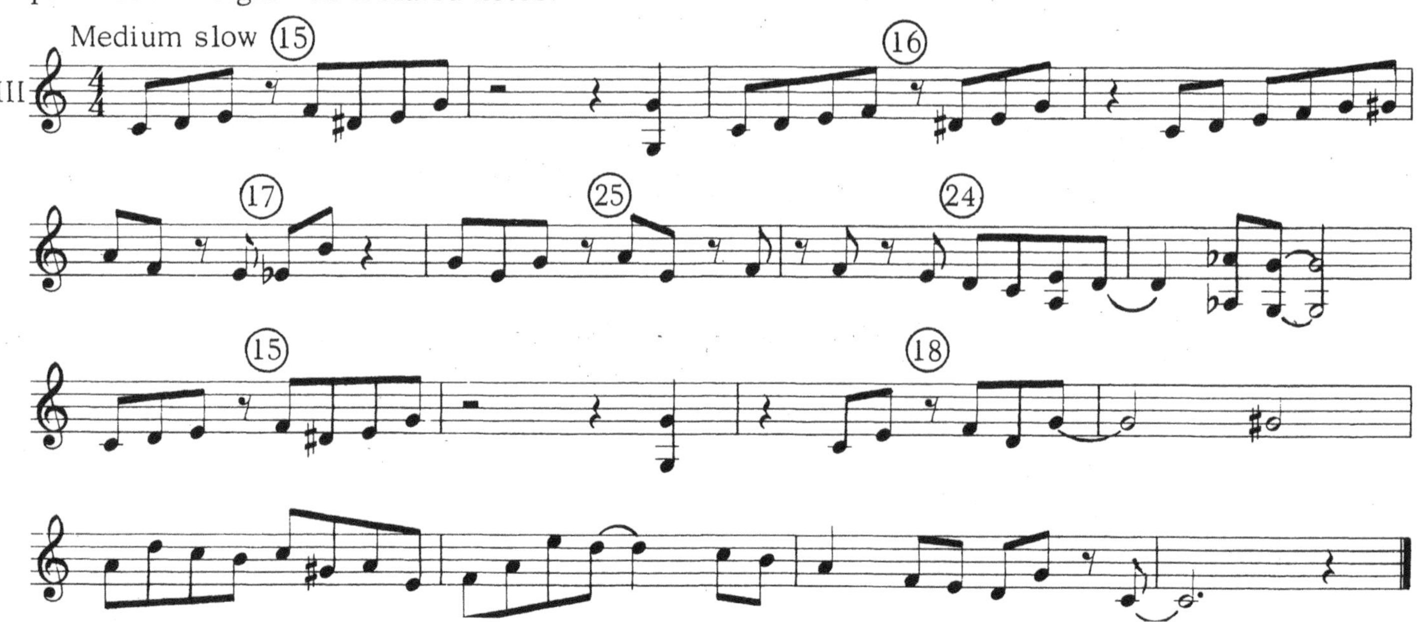

*Become familiar with different notations of the same figure.

Review each etude making smooth transitions from one figure to another. Play in a relaxed manner feeling eighth-note triplets (♩ 3 ♪) throughout.

REMEMBER: Whenever the *last eighth-note* of a figure falls on the *second part* of the *fourth beat* (4&) it is *accented* as an *"anticipated downbeat"* of the *following bar*.

SYNCOPATED QUARTERS AND EIGHTHS

(One bar figures)

*For fast reading, dance band music is often written so that the first and third (middle) beats can be recognized quickly.

FOUR ETUDES

(Syncopated quarters and eighths)

See Glossary (page 43) for tempo markings.

Use KEY (page 44) for difficult rhythms.

The number above each measure indicates the figure (on page 8) being used.

COMPREHENSIVE ETUDE

- One bar figures
- Syncopated quarters and eighths

Moderate

ONE BAR FIGURES EXTENDED

THREE ETUDES

(One bar figures extended)

The number over each measure indicates the figure (on page 11) being used.

COMPREHENSIVE ETUDE

One bar figures
Syncopated quarters and eighths
One bar figures extended

ANTICIPATIONS

Very often a syncopated (up-beat) note will anticipate the following down-beat to *start* a figure. Recall in one bar figures, anticipations came at the *end* of the bar.

[At this point the player should be familiar with quite a few dance band figures and their conception. All further examples will be explained *assuming* the basic "swing" eighth-note style. Check through the five basic rules again and remember to use both the Glossary and KEY as needed.]

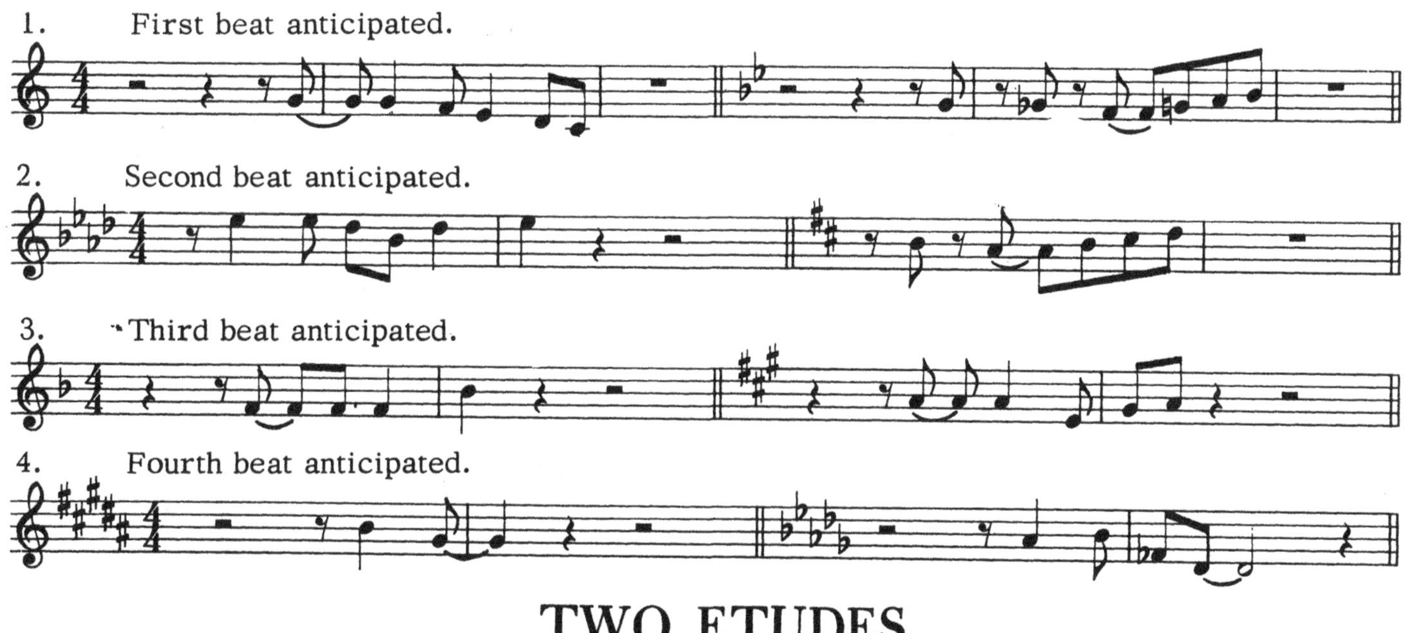

TWO ETUDES

(Anticipations)

The number over each measure shows *which beat* is *anticipated.*

I Moderate

① ① ② ③ ④ ④ ② ③

II Bright

③ ③ ④ ② ①

TWO BAR FIGURES

C and $\frac{4}{4}$ are identical and are used interchangeably.

TWO ETUDES

(Two bar figures)

The number over each measure indicates the *two bar figure* being used.

I

Moderate ④ ④ ⑤ ① ③ ⑧ ⑨ ⑬ ⑦

II

Medium bright ⑫ ⑭ ② ⑪ ⑥ ⑩

ETUDE

(Two bar figures anticipated)

THREE BAR FIGURES

TWO ETUDES

(Three bar figures)

The number over each measure indicates the three bar figure being used.

TWO REVIEW ETUDES

SINGLE NOTE PUNCTUATION

(See Glossary under "Punctuation" and "Tempo")

The one time a player "sticks out" over the whole band is when he mis-reads a punctuation figure. Practice the following figures and etudes carefully. Learn to "place" each note.

FOUR ETUDES

(Single note punctuation)

The number over each measure indicates the *punctuation figure* being used.

THREE REVIEW ETUDES

A good review of the preceeding pages from time to time, will help a great deal in becoming familiar with many of the most common dance figures. Learn to recognize and interpret these figures at first sight. Listen to good dance bands at every opportunity, and develop skill in hearing and recognizing the various figures. In listening, note any stylistic differences of a particular band in interpretation (longer quarter-notes, straight eighth-notes, accents, etc.).

When playing in a band *always* listen to, and phrase with, the lead player (first instrument of a section). Follow him *exactly* whether you agree with his interpretation or not. When you play lead, expect the *same* of the players in your section.

COMPREHENSIVE REVIEW ETUDE

DOTTED EIGHTH AND SIXTEENTH NOTE RHYTHMS

When in sequence, dotted eighth and sixteenth-notes are played *almost* the same as "swing eighth-notes". The *dotted eighth-note,* however, is usually played *short.*

When in sequence *and slurred*, dotted eighth and sixteenth-notes are played *exactly* the same as "swing eighth-notes".

When isolated (appearing once in a group of other notes) play with a *quick* sixteenth-note.

ETUDE

(Dotted eighth and sixteenth-note rhythms)

TRIPLETS

Eighth-note triplets are played "concert style" (*see* Glossary), and are usually played "legato"

Quarter-note triplets are also played legato, and in strict concert rhythm.

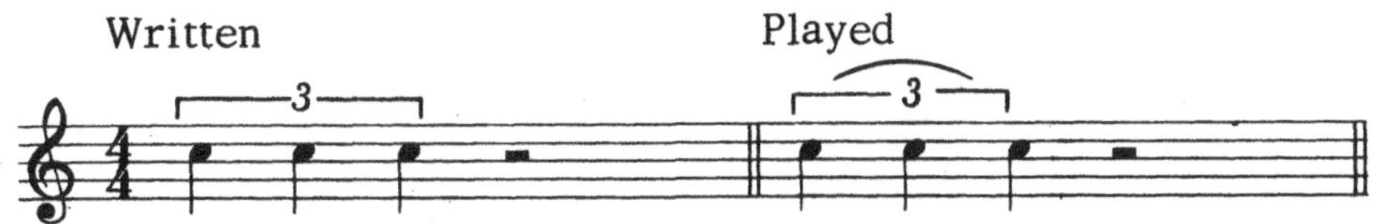

A dotted eighth and sixteenth-note figure followed by a triplet, is played with a short dotted eighth-note, and a quick sixteenth-note, slurred to the first note of the triplet.

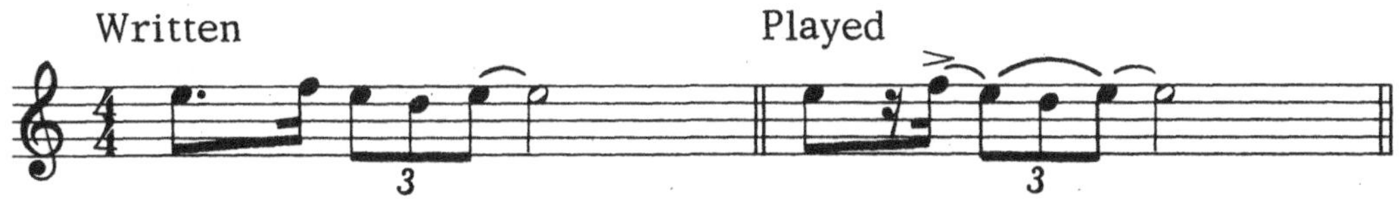

ETUDE

(Triplets with dotted eighth and sixteenth-notes)

Medium slow

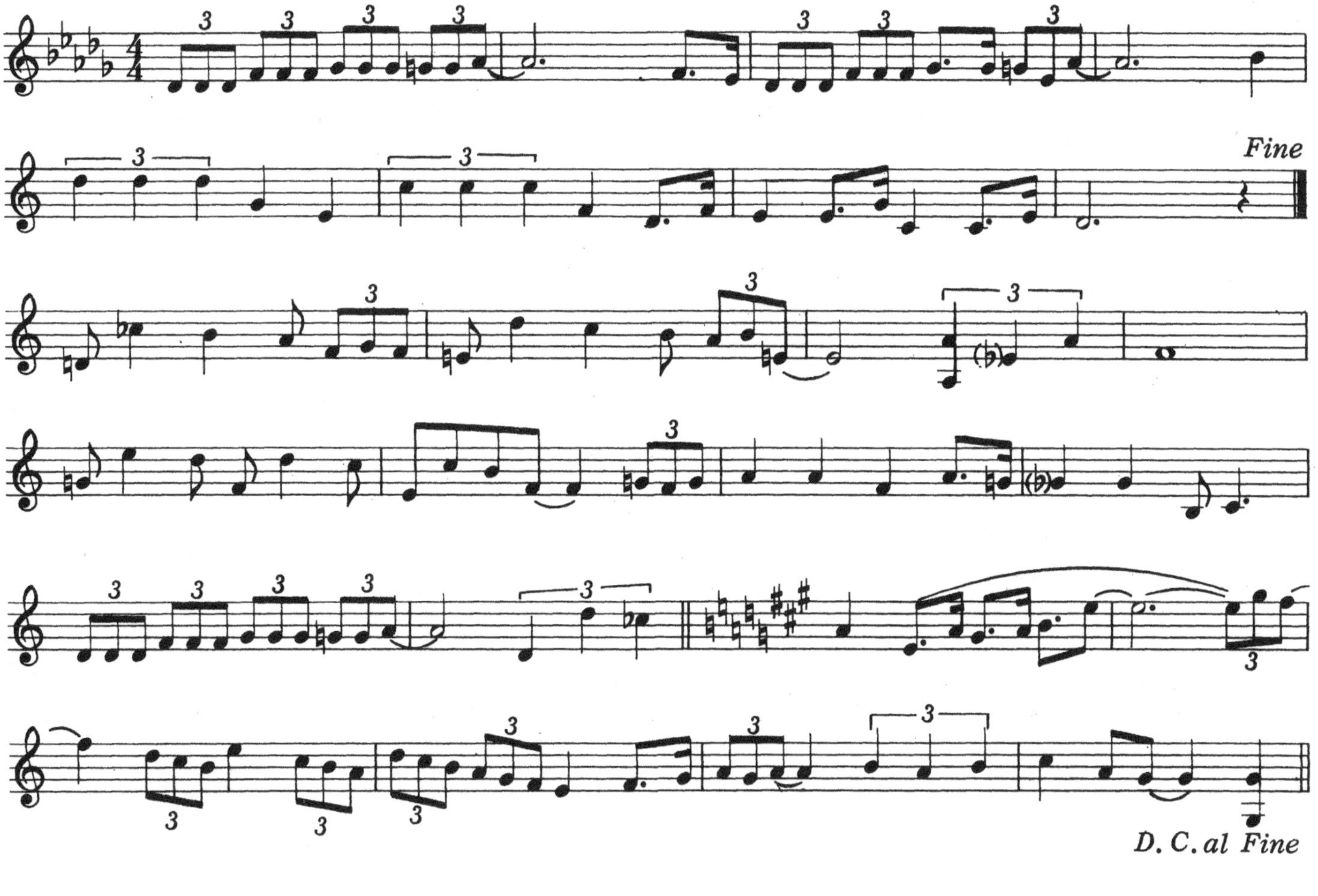

Fine

D. C. al Fine

SIXTEENTH NOTES

Four sixteenth-notes in a row are played legato and even (concert style).

An eighth-note followed by two sixteenth-notes is played short. The two sixteenth-notes are quick and lead to the next note.

Two sixteenth-notes followed by an eighth-note are played quick (leading to the eighth-note which is played short). The eighth-note should be played exactly in the middle of the beat (concert style).

When playing *lines* of eighth-notes and sixteenth-notes, roll the eighth-notes and play the sixteenth-notes even.

A sixteenth-note followed by an eighth-note, and another sixteenth-note, is played by slurring the first sixteenth-note into a short eighth-note. The second sixteenth-note is also slurred into whatever follows.

ETUDE

(Sixteenth-note rhythms)

DOUBLE TIME

Within an arrangement in a medium slow 4, there often is a "double time" section where the rhythm doubles its beat and each bar in $\frac{4}{4}$ "feels" like 2 bars in $\frac{4}{8}$.

Each type of note is played as though it were a note twice its value.

One bar in double time should sound the same as two bars in a bright tempo.

EXAMPLE:

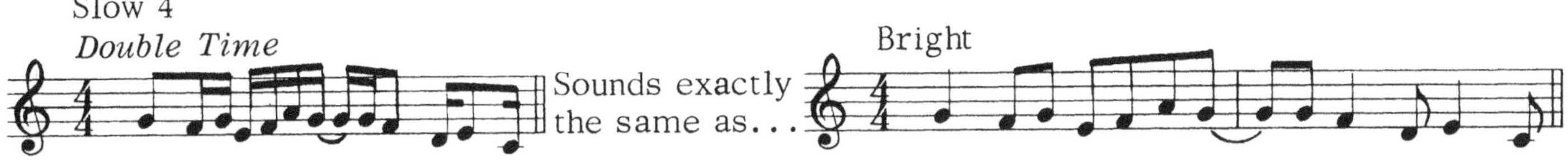

DOUBLE TIME EXAMPLE

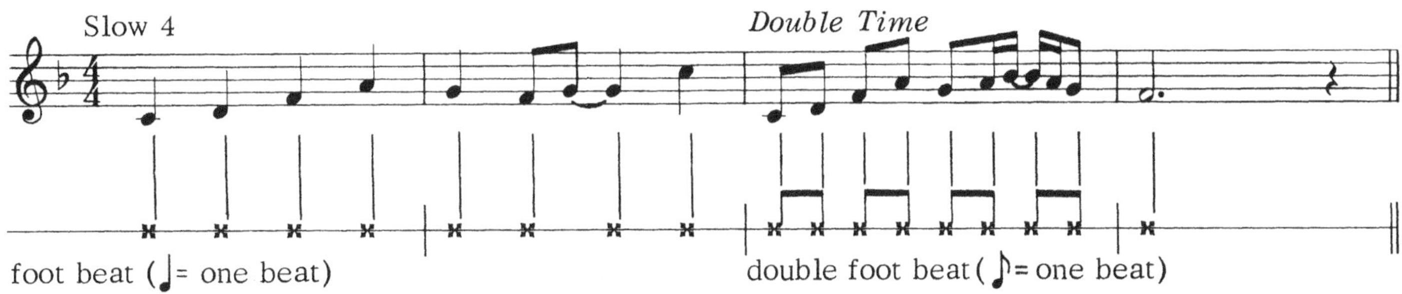

ETUDE

(Double time)

CUT TIME ¢

Cut time indicates 2 beats in a $\frac{4}{4}$ bar. The *half note* gets one beat.

Notes on the up-beat are *strongly accented.*

Written Played

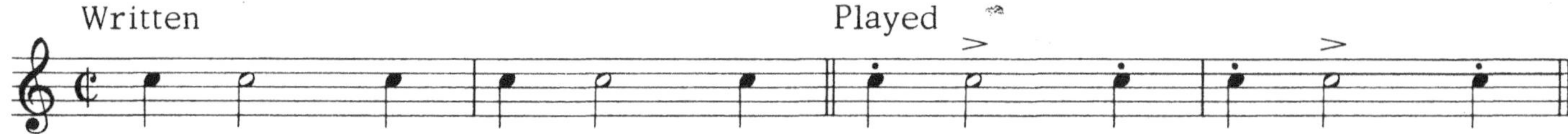

Figures with eighth-notes follow the regular rules, but are usually *clipped short.*

Written Played

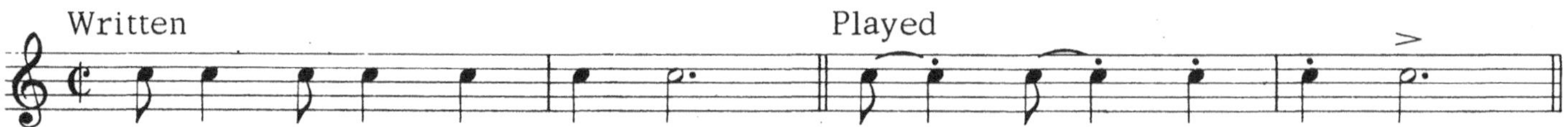

CUT TIME FIGURES

1.

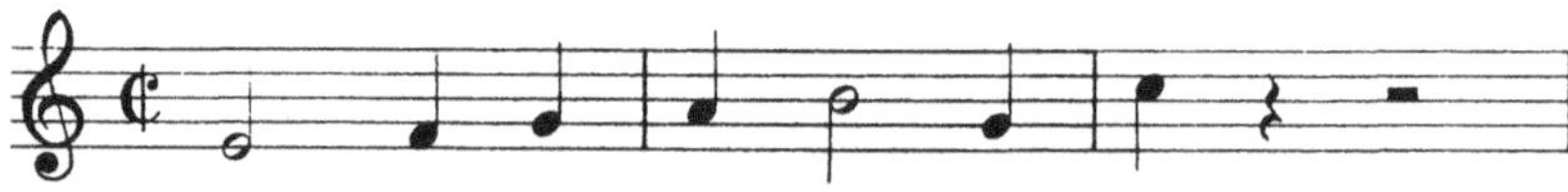

2.

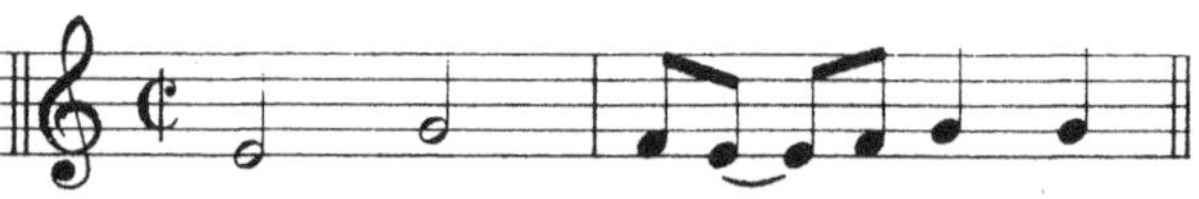

3.

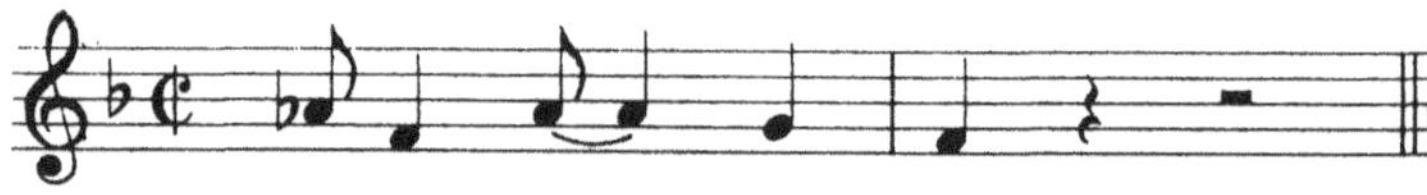

4.

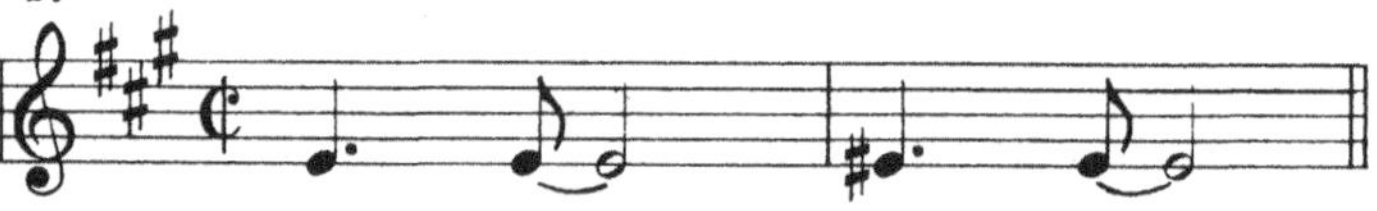

5.

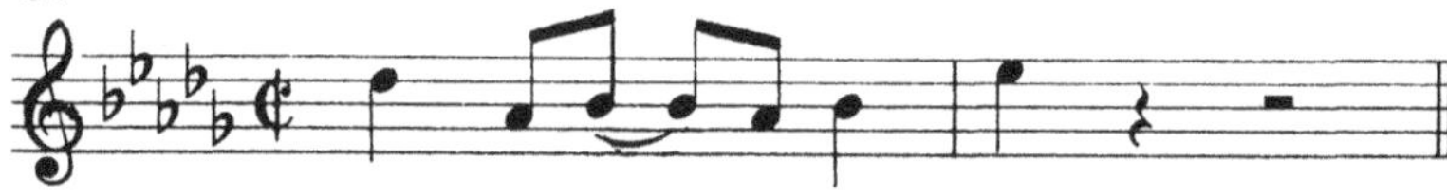

6.

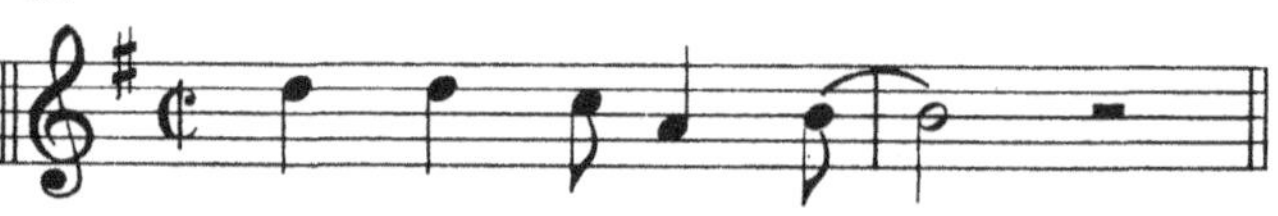

7.

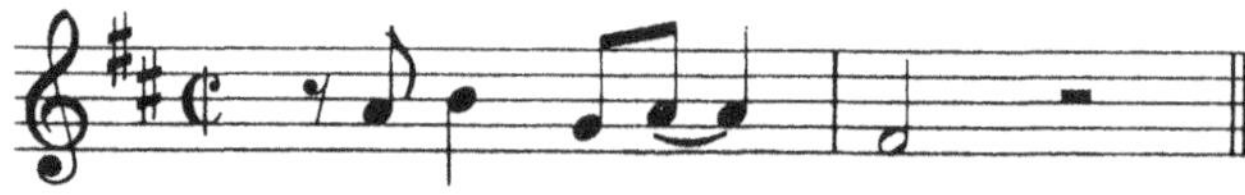

8.

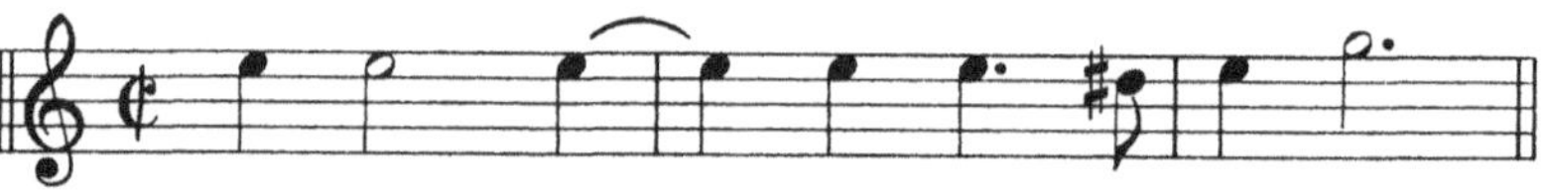

9.

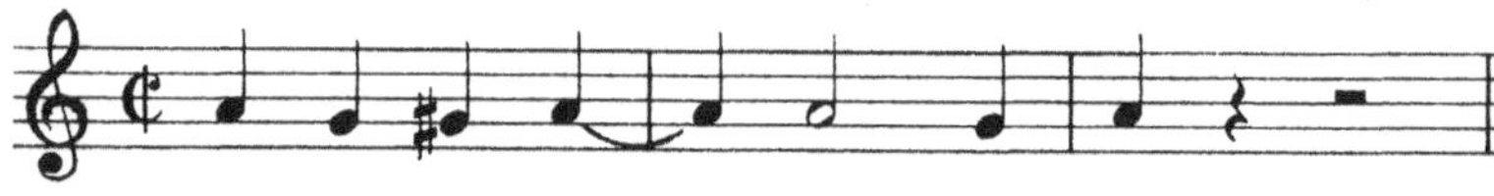

10.

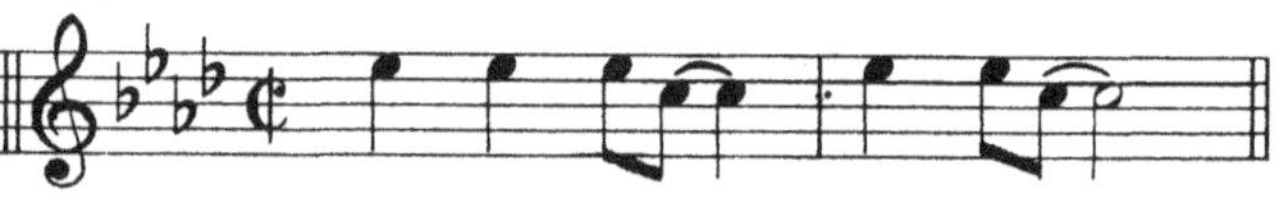

11.

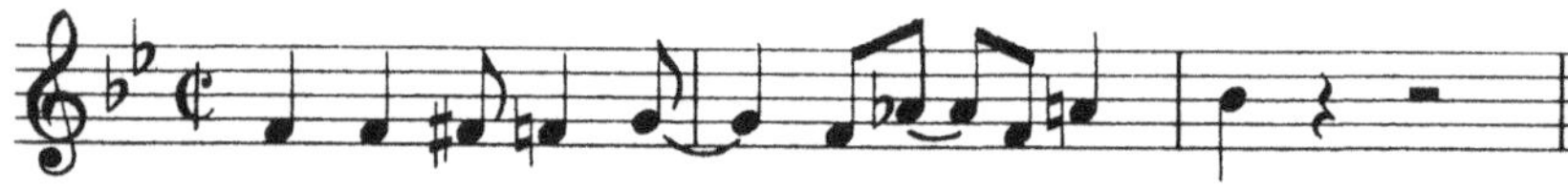

12.

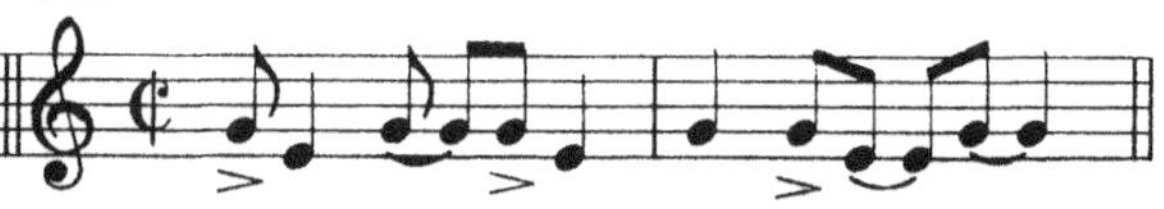

13.

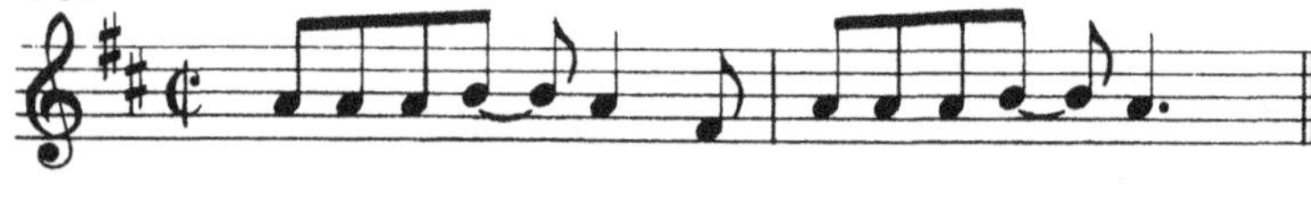

14.

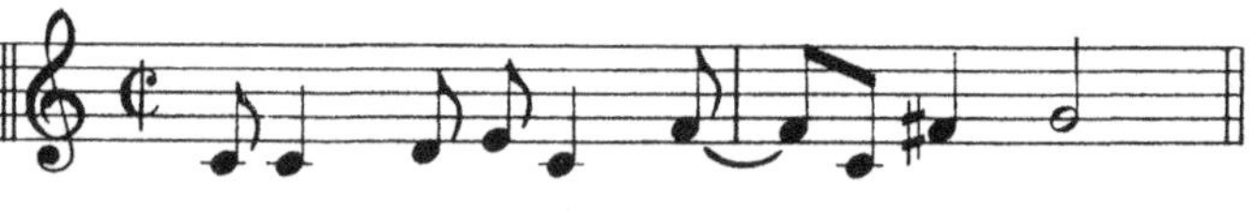

ETUDE

(Cut time)

The number over each measure indicates the *cut time figure* being used.

HALF TIME

Half time is the direct *opposite* of Double time (see p. 25). Half time occurs in an up tempo (fast) arrangement, where for a period of time (often toward the end) the rhythm "halves" its beat and becomes a slow heavy swing. Each bar in $\frac{4}{4}$ becomes one half of a bar in $\frac{4}{2}$.

Each type of note is played as though it were a note half its value.

Written - Played

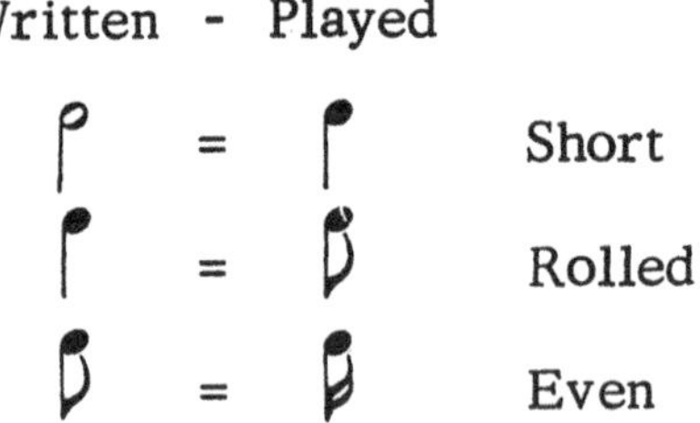

EXAMPLE:

Fast 4

Half Time ("Roll" the quarter-notes)

foot beat (♩= one beat)

"half" foot beat (𝅗𝅥= one beat)

ETUDE

(Half time)

Fast 4

Half time

Regular time

SPECIAL MARKINGS

EXCEPTIONS TO BASIC RULES

SPECIAL

WRITTEN / SOUNDS	BRASS	REEDS (SAXOPHONE)
RIP (FLARE)	 Start before the beat and run three or four notes *up* to the main note.	Start before the beat and run three or four notes *up* to the main note.
FALL-OFF	 Play main note strong and scatter fall-off notes with a decrescendo.	Play main note strong and scatter fall-off notes with a decrescendo.
 GLISSANDO (Gliss.)	Use half-valve; creating a smooth sound from one note to the other.	Down Gliss: light chromatic scale. Up Gliss: half-hole or, fingered notes aided by lip.
SMEAR	 Lip main note "flat" and bring up to pitch. (Or use half-valve.)	Lip main note "flat" (loose embouchere) and bring up to pitch.
TURN	 Play first note and "fall down" to 2nd note from one or two overtones* above.	Play first note and "fall down" to 2nd note from one or two notes higher (in key).
SHAKE (TRILL)	 Lip trill note with one overtone higher, or shake horn (rougher sound).	Fast trill with keys from written note to one tone higher.
BEND 	Play as shown in example.	Play as shown in example.
DROP	 Drop from higher overtone to written note.	Start before the beat and run five or six notes *down* to written note.
IMPLIED NOTE	 Finger the implied note but play it much softer than the other notes.	Finger the implied note but play it much softer than the other notes.
SQUEEZE (PORTAMENTO) (Squeeze)	 Similar to Gliss. but notes in between should be heard less distinctly.	Similar to Gliss. but notes in between should be heard less distinctly.
DOIT	 Half-valve and lip to about an octave above written note.	Play fast scale to note about an octave above the written note.
CLOSED-OPEN (+ o +o / Doo Dah Doo-wah / closed open close-open)	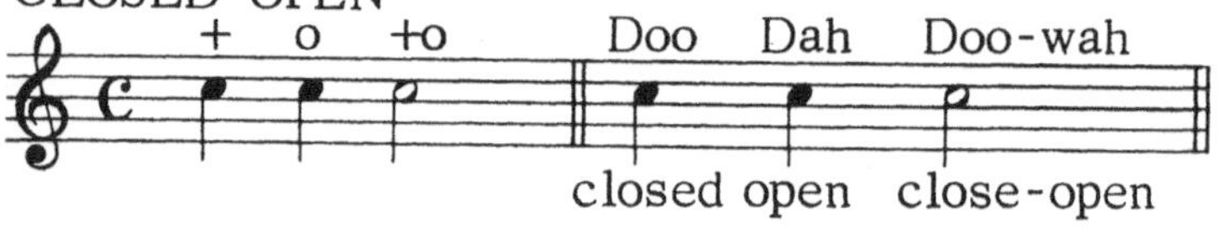 + Hand over Bell o Hand away from Bell.	+ Bite hard to close note. o Open to free note.

*Overtones are the various notes that can be produced with the lip alone in one valve setting on brass instruments.

EFFECTS

STRINGS (GUITAR)
Start before the beat and run three or four notes *up* to the main note.
Play main note strong and scatter fall-off notes with a decrescendo.
Slide finger along the fingerboard for the 2nd note.
Slide along fingerboard from half-tone below to main note.
Play first note and "fall down" to 2nd note from one or two notes higher (in key).
Trill note with one tone higher.
Play as shown in example.
Play like fast Glissando *down* to written note.
Play implied note lightly. (Guitar, finger but don't pluck the implied note.)
Same as Glissando.
Slide along fingerboard to note about one octave above the written note.
+ Press finger lightly on string. o Normal Pressure. (or; play "+" *lightly*.)

USED IN CONTEXT

OTHER SPECIAL EFFECTS

The following effects should be used at the player's own discretion when playing a solo, or lead part in an ensemble.

1. FLUTTER TONGUE - Roll tongue like a Spanish "R" - (Trrrrr).

2. GROWL - Use throat growl like a French "R".

3. THROAT HUM - Hum deep in throat while playing a note, this gives the tone a "rough" quality.

4. ALTERNATE FINGERING - Repeated notes on Brass or Reed instruments are often played with an alternate or "false" fingering on every other note.

5. HALF-VALVE - (Brass) - Used frequently for Rips, Fall-offs, Doits, Glissandos, etc. Press valves halfway down.

6. HALF-HOLE - (Open Hole Reeds: clarinet, flute, etc.) Use in a similar manner to half-valve on brass instruments for Glissandos, Squeezes, Doits, Smears, etc. Cover a portion of the open hole with finger and then slide open. Use on several holes for "true" Glissando upwards.

ETUDE
(Special effects)

TEN FINAL DANCE ETUDES

Note various effects through use of Dynamics.

I

Medium slow

II

Apply the same rules as in 4/4.
III
Moderate (in 1)
3

IV

V

Same tempo from $\frac{3}{4}$ to $\frac{4}{4}$. (feel the $\frac{3}{4}$ bars in 1 and the $\frac{4}{4}$ bars in a fast 4.)

Bright

VI

Note irregular (7, 9, etc. bar) phrases.

VII

VIII

Moderate

IX

Many arrangements also "swing" in irregular meters.

X

GLOSSARY

Bar	Measure
Comprehensive etude	A study in which all of the important features of a lesson are contained.
Concert style	Straight meter; exact note values: each quarter-note is divided into two equal eighth-notes.
Down beat (Up beat)	Down beats are on the numbers (1, 2, 3, 4). Up beats are on the &s (1&, 2&, 3&, 4&). Down Up 1 & 2 & 3 & 4 & 1 & 2 & 3 & 4 &
Dynamics	Volume markings (*pp*, *p*, *mp*, *mf*, *f*, *ff*).
Eighth-note triplets	(*See* "rolled eighth-notes" below.)
Etude	A study; with musical form and direction.
Figure	A rhythmic statement or pattern (short or long).
Impulse	Any one of the eight rolled eighth-notes that underlie each bar of regular metered dance band music.
Legato	Smooth; slurred.
Markings	Markings in dance band music are basically the same as those found in concert music. > sharp attack and decline. ^ heavy. — long. . short. ⌒ slur or tie. , breath. < crescendo (louder). > decrescendo or diminuendo (softer).
Part	The music that one instrument reads from.
Punctuation	Short rhythmic accents to highlight various impulses of a bar. Often used by one section of a band, while a melody is being played by another section, to create rhythmic excitement.
Rolled eighth-notes	Eighth-note triplets, with the first two notes tied. The basis for interpreting dance band music.
Swing eighth-notes	Same as rolled eighth-notes (*see* above).
Syncopation	Figures involving accented up beats.
Tempo markings	Approximate metronome markings: Slow, Slow heavy, Medium slow: ♩=50 - 72 (longer notes, heavy accents, more weight on notes.) Medium, Moderate, Moderate lift, Medium bright: ♩=72 - 144 Bright, Bright 2, Fast, Very fast: ♩=144 - 208 (eighth-notes become more even, punctuation figures tend to be played in more of a concert style, shorter notes, lighter accents.)
Time	Regular: $\frac{4}{4}$, $\frac{3}{4}$, $\frac{2}{4}$, $\frac{6}{8}$ Cut: $\frac{4}{4}=\frac{2}{2}$ Double: $\frac{4}{4}=\frac{8}{8}$ or $\frac{4}{8}+\frac{4}{8}$ Half: $\frac{4}{4}=\frac{2}{2}+\frac{2}{2}$ Stop:
Up beat	(*See* "down beat" above).

KEY

(Eight "swing" eighth-notes to the bar)

In order to interpret the rhythm of difficult figures:

1. Place an "X" for each separate note of the figure on the appropriate line of the diagram.

Example: (one bar figures #5)

2. Beat a constant "swing" eighth-note rhythm with the hand and sing each "X" as it occurs.

Leave lines blank wherever rests occur.

For quarter-notes, place "X" and leave the next line blank.

If part of the figure has a note longer than a quarter-note (or two tied eighth-notes) draw a line after the initial "X" through all the beats it covers.

Example: (one bar figures #13)

Use this KEY for 1 through 4 bar phrases.

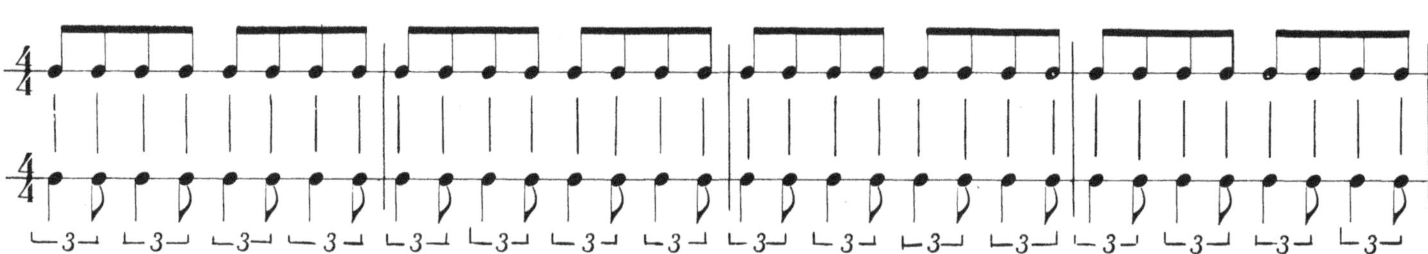

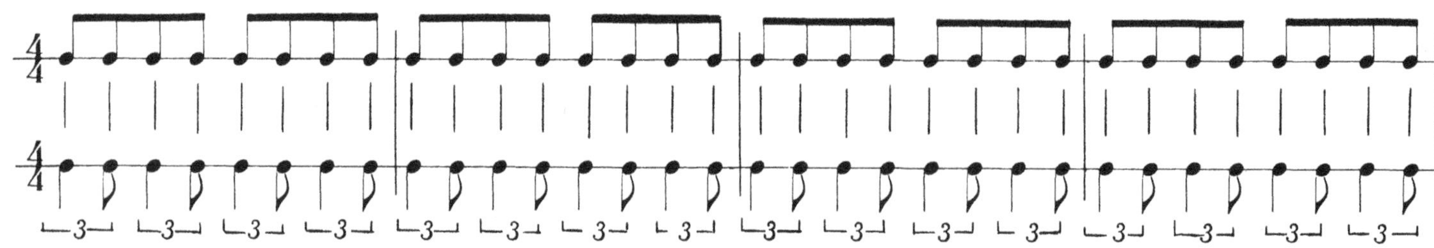

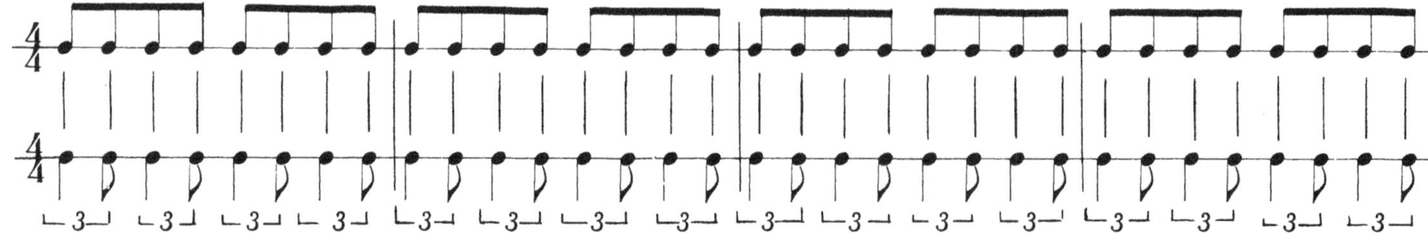